LIAR
Lie Detection Made Easy
1st Edition

by
Trent Pettigrew

Contents

INTRODUCTION 3
CH 1 WHAT THIS BOOK IS 12
CH 2 MINDSET 16
CH 3 LAYING THE FOUNDATION 21
CH 4 THE MOST IMPORTANT CHAPTER IN THIS BOOK 33
CH 5 RED FLAG WORDS AND PHRASES 57
CH6 TOP TEN INDICATORS OF A LIAR 65
CH 7 BODY LANGUAGE 68
CH 8 REVIEW 80
CLOSING 93
ABOUT THE AUTHOR 96

Introduction

Let's face it, you have possibly attended a body language or statement analysis class/seminar/book/video and been led to believe that you can tell if a person is being truthful or deceptive by their eye movements, body movements, etc. You may have also been taught about proxemics, linguistics, and all kinds of other fancy jargon to determine if someone is being truthful or deceptive. The bottom line is that although these techniques can help determine truthfulness or deception, they require years of education and/or frequent use, they can be very complicated, and they are by no means fool-proof. In some cases, they are not even accurate or reliable.

It is also quite possible that you have been taught these classes by someone who has a big fancy education or has been taught all of this "lie detection" information in countless classes, but has absolutely zero "real world" experience. Would you go to a doctor who learned about heart surgery in a book, yet had never done a surgery, or would you go to a doctor that not only studied and learned heart surgery, but also performed the surgeries he had learned on a weekly or daily basis for years? Only each individual can answer that question, but you can bet your butt, I want the guy who has "been there, done that!"

The purpose of the LIAR book is to teach you real-world techniques for determining truthfulness or deception. This book is for the common man, woman, mom, dad, business person, etc. This is a book for "the rest of us." I know the information contained in this book works for Law Enforcement. I know it works in an Interview Room and on the side of the road in the middle of nowhere, but that's not the goal of this book. My goal is to teach you what works in everyday life and conversation, not what works for Law Enforcement or in a classroom. I have been practicing these techniques for almost 20 years and teaching these techniques for approximately 15 years. I know that what is contained in this book works. It's up to you what's done with the information. Use it and you'll have an advantage over others. Whether buying a car, making a business deal, confronting a cheating spouse, or determining who stole a cookie, you will have the advantage of knowing the truth, or at least who's NOT telling the truth!

This book will teach you simple techniques, red flag words and phrases, and simple solutions to use in real world, day-to-day life. I am also throwing in a bonus chapter toward the end of the book that will help enhance the techniques that you have learned in the book, but this book is in no way a "body language" book. The bottom line and main focus of this book will be to determine deception based upon what people say. You will be taught that everything a person says has a meaning, and our job will be to listen to what people are "really" saying. The one thing that will be concentrated on in this book is that "people's words will betray them." People can learn to control their body language, their proxemics, etc., but their words will slip up on them and we will learn to take advantage of this weakness.

There are two kinds of behavior. Verbal behavior is the words that are actually spoken and the choice of words used. This is the area that we will concentrate on. Non-verbal behavior consists of facial expressions and body movements used to express the words that are chosen.

Studies have determined the dominant communication between individuals is the non-verbal, accounting for between 55% to 65% of communication between individuals. Between 30% to 40% of communication is done using tone of voice. Less than 10% of communication between people is the actual result of words that are spoken. However, this small 10% of communication is where 90% of lie detection occurs! You cannot tell if someone is lying to you unless you hear their words, or see their words in writing. Words are the key to determining deception. Are we really smart enough to stand there and watch someone's body language and hear a slight change in tone of voice and still determine if they are lying or not? Hell, high tech machines are not even able to determine this! Not only that, but these high tech machines are so unreliable and unproven that they are not even admissible in a court of law!

Here's the beauty of the information in this book. Even the least educated of us can determine if someone is lying simply from the result of the WORDS they have spoken to us! Not only that, but they don't even have to be present for us to know that we are being lied to. You can determine deception while speaking on the phone, listening to the radio, or reading a person's written statement. That's a HUGE advantage over body language!

It is my hope that you will glean some valuable information from this book that you can use for the rest of your life. I know you will be pleasantly surprised!

CHAPTER 1

WHAT THIS BOOK IS

This book is simply a guide and a collection of lie detection techniques that I know work. This book and the information contained within is by no means an "end all, be all" on lie detection. Inevitably there will be someone who states, "that's too simple, there is way more to lie detection." Yes there is more, but my goal is to make lie detection as easy, uncomplicated, and efficient as possible for the common man or woman in everyday life. We're not going to get bogged down with "trying" to read people's eye movements, looking for a movement in someone's foot, or detecting a slight change in someone's "tone" of voice. That crap is not "real world," and therefore, we're not going to concentrate on it. I just recently read a "lie detection" book that looked and read like a damn math book! Hell, I'm somewhat educated and it scrambled my brain after the first chapter! Needless to say, if there was any good information in the book, I missed out. I'm sitting here looking at it collecting dust on my bookshelf as I write this.

This book is also my "gift" and response to all of my co-workers who have asked me to write a book, teach their "Troop" a class, or have asked me what my secret to lie detection is. Maybe more importantly is that this book is my response to those who ask me what I think the most important facet of lie detection is or what they should study in order to improve their ability to detect deception. This, my friends, is it! This book is the foundation, the basics and the fundamentals, that must be mastered in order to be built upon. This book contains, in my opinion, the most important aspects of lie detection. Anything past this is just icing on the cake. Just like stance, balance, and relaxation are important fundamentals of sports, this book contains the important fundamentals of lie detection.

It has been said that an average person who has studied jiu jitsu for one year, can defeat more than 80% of people on the planet in a street fight. While that information may be debatable, one thing is not. If you learn and apply the information in this book, you will have an advantage over 80% of people on the planet in regards to detecting deception and lies. Folks, that is something of value that no one can take from you!

I do ask one thing from the reader of this book. Don't judge the information and techniques presented too quickly. Some, if not most of this information, will seem too easy to work and be effective. I assure you, it works! Give it time and you'll be amazed at the ease of which you will be able to detect deception. The more you become aware, the more you will chuckle at the information and advantage you will gain over others.

The sad part is, you will see how truly evil and deceptive this world is, but, we all live in this world and must arm ourselves with the tools to survive in it.

CHAPTER 2

MINDSET

Okay, there are a few things that need to be understood before we get into this book.

Anyone and everyone will lie to you! If you think a preacher, teacher, cop, attorney, doctor, or politician will not lie to you, you really need to step back and re-evaluate a few things. Absolutely these people will lie to you! You cannot let your preconceived ideas of who is honest and who is not interfere with the task at hand. Everyone will, or is capable of, lying to you! Always remember that!

If you don't really want to know the truth on a sensitive subject, don't read the book. If you think people won't lie to you and that most people are honest and would never mislead another person, don't read the book. My advice would be to continue on in your world of lucky charms and unicorns. Hey, I wish the world was like that, but we must be realistic about the type of world that we live in. This is a cold, hard world, with plenty of folks with bad intentions and deception on their mind. The information in this book will allow you to wade through the oceans of deceit and protect yourself and your interests. Detecting deception will never go out of style or become outdated!

In a world full of fads and one-hit wonders that come and go, lying, cheating, and deception will always remain constant. In fact, it is my belief that it gets worse as time goes on. It's been here since biblical times and will remain until the end of times. Don't believe that lies and deceit are a big deal? Let's see what the bible advises on the matter:

Do Not Lie (Leviticus 19:11)

Not a word from their mouth can be trusted; with their tongue they speak deceit (Psalm 5:9)

Keep your lips from speaking lies (Psalm 34:13)

Rescue me from liars and all deceitful people (Psalm 120:2)

The Lord detests lying lips (Proverbs 12:22)

A liar will be destroyed (Proverbs 19:9)

A liar will not go unpunished (Proverbs 101:7)

Truthful words stand the test of time, but lies are soon exposed (Proverbs 12:19)

These verses aren't even close to the tip

of the iceberg regarding the quotes about lying in the bible. Obviously, lying and deception have been major issues since the beginning of time (remember Adam and Eve) and will continue to be until the end of time. Arm yourself with the knowledge to decipher truth from deceit! What a valuable asset to have!

I'm not sure if this will give you any assurance or not, but I have used these techniques on a daily basis for almost 20 years. I still do. Early on in my career, I was trained mostly in body language, and I thought it was the only way to read someone. I was WRONG! I was missing the mark. The more training I received and the more I used the information at work, the more I realized the real game was in people's words and statements! Folks, I'm telling you, this is where it's at. It's so easy, it doesn't seem right. Learn the contents of this book, and you will have a tactical and strategic advantage over others! Period!

CHAPTER 3

LAYING THE FOUNDATION

Word and Statement Lie Detection is the process of analyzing a person's words to reveal if that person is being truthful or deceptive. This provides you with the additional information of knowing exactly what the person is saying.

Once again, an advantage of this form of lie detection is that you do not need to see the person, hear the person, or even know anything about the person in order to determine if the person is being truthful. This means you can use this technique on the telephone, while listening to an audio recording, or while reading a written statement.

The two greatest advantages to Lie Detection through Verbal or Written

Statements:

1. As you listen to or read someone's statement, you need to know if the person is being truthful. This is especially true if you are conducting an interview. If the subject is misleading you, and you do not realize this information, you will conclude the interview having obtained little information and perhaps bad information.

2. There are times that someone will tell us one thing, but we hear something different. This is because we have the tendency to interpret what people are saying. However, you should never *interpret,* because people mean exactly what they are saying! By paying attention to each word used in the statement, you are able to recognize what a person is saying and gain additional information from the subject.

Peoples words will betray them if you will listen!

It is not easy to withhold information. Even a deceptive person who is doing their best to withhold information will tell us more than they realize. Unfortunately, people sometimes tell us more than what WE realize. The key is to listen to what people are saying and to know what to listen for in their answers.

The truth WILL slip out. If a person is lying, their deception will normally appear several times throughout their answers in various ways. These clues are something that we want to look and listen for in order to determine truthfulness or deception. However, there are times when deception may only be one single word! Therefore, we must pay careful attention to everything the person says!

True Stories Come From Memory

A truthful story comes from memory and should freely flow from the subject. It's similar to watching a movie and telling you what is happening.

A deceptive story comes from imagination. The person cannot rely completely on their memory to tell you what happened. They have to partially construct their story as they tell it. They will usually show signs that they are thinking about what to say instead of reliving the events in their mind. They will usually stumble with words, pause, and even contradict something they previously said.

Remember, there are also "little things" that happen during events (crying baby, birds singing, etc.) that should be found somewhere within the true story.

The Shortest Answer Is The Best Answer

(I cannot stress enough the importance of this one!)

When answering a specific question, a truthful person will normally give a short, straightforward answer. They do not need to explain themselves because they have told you the truth.

A deceptive person will find it hard to directly answer a question if it is going to incriminate them. They may include additional words in their answer, such as qualifying words (for example: maybe, might have, could have, probably, I can't remember.)

Everything a Person Says has a Meaning

A person may provide you with information that appears to have little or nothing to do with your questions. There is a reason they gave the information! Your job is to find out why they added the information!

People Do Not Want To Lie

(Believe it! I didn't early in my career, I do now!)

In an open answer in which a person can say anything they want, most people will not tell a lie. The reason people choose not to knowingly lie is that it causes stress.

Another reason people will not lie in an open answer is that they do not know what you know (Use this to your advantage! This is a very powerful advantage for you!) If they tell you a lie and you have proof it is a lie, then they are in trouble. So, the safest way for them to play it is to not tell any lies.

Despite their truthfulness, a subject may neglect to tell you some crucial and perhaps incriminating information. Therefore, you also need to look at what the subject HAS NOT told you! (Important)

If a person says, "I didn't do it" believe them. They probably didn't do it. Guilty people rarely sat "I didn't do it." If a person says, "I wouldn't do that" believe him. HOWEVER, recognize that the person HAS NOT told you that they didn't do it! The same applies if the person says, "I couldn't do that." Belief in the person helps you to recognize exactly what the person is saying and it provides you with additional information.

The Denial

When people are accused of doing something they should not have done, they will often deny it. Many guilty people will not deny committing a crime. They will give you an answer that sounds like a denial, but the reality is that they have not denied committing the act itself.

You may hear responses like these, but keep in mind, these are NOT innocent responses!

"I am innocent."

"I am not guilty."

"I couldn't have done that."

"I wouldn't have done that."

"I had nothing to do with..."

"I deny..."

There is one example in particular that I like to use to drive this point home. Being a proud Oklahoman and being sent to assist during the Murrah Bombing in Oklahoma City, I closely followed the interviews and information surrounding Timothy McVeigh. McVeigh and his attorney were interviewed while McVeigh was in jail. The interviewer asked, "Did you bomb the Murrah building?" McVeigh answered with the following statement. "The only way we can really answer that is we are going to plead not guilty."

Now ask yourself, is that the ONLY way you could answer that question? How about, "I didn't do it." Don't you think it could have been answered that way? Hell yes it could have been answered that way, and should have been, had he been innocent. However, I think we all know McVeigh was less than innocent on this occasion...We can all thank a brave, eagle eyed Oklahoma State Trooper for that statement analysis lesson!

Here is what you ARE looking for:
"I didn't do it."

When a person says, "I didn't do it", they are denying the act. They are telling us that they did not commit the crime, or they did not commit a certain act. The only true denial is to state "I didn't do it"!!! (Important)

"I am innocent" = Deny the conclusion
"I didn't do it" = Deny the act

It is a well-known fact that innocent people tend to answer questions differently than people who are lying. Being aware of what a person says and how they say it may provide clues as to whether they are deceptive or not. A few examples are:

1. Liars try to minimize their actions
2. Liars try to blame the crime on the

victim

3. Liars may blame the action on a phantom that no one else saw
4. Liars may claim unreliable memories
5. Liars may not make strong, immediate denials to insinuations that there is evidence linking them to a crime
6. Liars may use "reinforcing" statements to back up their assertions of truthfulness ("I swear to God...") I will provide a list of these key phrases later in the book
7. Liars denials tend to grow weaker over the course of an interview, while innocent people tend to get stronger in their denials
8. Liars do not exhibit the normal strength of emotion that innocent people do

Learning this information takes some time and practice, but what a great tool in your toolbox!!!

CHAPTER 4

THE MOST IMPORTANT CHAPTER IN THIS BOOK

Matthew 5:37

Simply let your "Yes" be "Yes", and your "No" be "No", anything beyond this comes from evil.

As the chapter heading states, I believe this is the most important chapter of this book, of any book, that is designed to teach lie detection. Even though the information in this book is easy to digest, always refer to this little chapter if you are ever in need of a little "refresher" or reminder of the basics. As you'll see, it's not rocket science, but it is extremely effective!

Okay, let's jump right into this, but let's keep one thing in mind: there are not many absolutes in life, and the same goes for detecting deception in the spoken word. Do not take one indicator standing alone as a definite sign of deception. However, several indicators clustered together are always good!!! If it looks like a duck, walks like a duck, and quacks like a duck, it's a DUCK!!! The same applies for Liars!!!

With that said, let's define a lie. What is a lie? **A lie is a deliberate choice to mislead someone without giving notification or intent.**

Why do people lie? **People lie for self-preservation.** (Very Important)

You cannot assign different values to lies. A lie is a lie, Period!!! There is no such thing as a little white lie or a harmless lie. Someone is lying to you for a reason, and it's up to you to figure out why!!!

You must also remember different ways to lie. Som just bold face lie to you, or he or she could lie by leaving out important facts or pertinent information. Believe it or not, given the chance, most people would prefer NOT to lie. It is up to you to ask the direct questions that force that person into coming clean with the truth, or lying.

Now that we've defined a lie, let's get to what I believe is the most important word in lie detection: **Reticence!**

Reticence: Does the answer equal the question you asked???

This gets straight to the heart of the Matthew 5:37 quote.

Let your "Yes" be "Yes", and your "No"

No."

Example: Question - "Mr. Usedcarsalesman, has this car ever been wrecked?"

Answer – "You know, this is a really clean car and we have all of the service records. If we've serviced the car, you know it has been well cared for!"

Did Mr. UCS answer the question? Hell No! The answer should have simply been Yes or No!!! It really is that simple and it follows the reticence rule – does the answer equal the question you asked?

Example: Question – "Son, we are

missing two cookies from the cookie jar. Did you take the cookies?"

Answer – "Ummm, I didn't..."

Did the son answer the question? Nope! Should have been a yes or no. However, after looking a little closer at his answer, do you think the son took the cookies?

If you're thinking no, he didn't take the cookies, but he knows who did, you are in the game and paying attention to the words!!!!

Example: Question – "Mr. Probaseballplayer, have you ever used steroids in your baseball career?"

Answer – "I would like to keep my answers positive and concentrate on the future, not the past..."

Did Mr. PBP follow the reticence rule? Hell No! This was a simple yes or no question. Let your "Yes" be "Yes" and your "No" be "No"!

Mr. PBP did not come out and bold face lie, he lied by not answering the question. Mr. PBP is a liar, and he used steroids while playing baseball. Simple as that!

Q. "Jon, are you having an affair on me?"

A. "Honey, I love you. Why would you even ask that?"

Did Jon answer the question? No! I think we know the answer on this one! In questions like this, another common response of the deceptive person is to act upset and blame the person who asked the question.

Q. "Brian, have you ever used steroids?"

A. "Whatever dude", and walks off.

Did Brian answer the question? No! Looks like Brian has, or is, using steroids!!!

Q. Son, we are concerned about you possibly using drugs. "Do you have any cocaine in your backpack?"

A. "No"

Q. "Do you have any meth in your

backpack?"

A. "No"

Q. "Do you have any marijuana in your backpack?"

A. "I'm not a drug dealer!"

The first two questions followed the reticence rule, what about the third? No! Any guess on what drugs you'll find in his backpack? If you said marijuana, you would be right!

Q. "Mary, are you having an affair with your boss?"

A. "Noooooo, No, No, No, No, I would never do that!"

Why all the no's? A simple "no" would

suffice. Mary is trying way too hard to convince us of her innocence. Mary would "never" do that? Let's be realistic!!! In the immortal words of Shakespeare ,"Me thinks thoust do protest too much!"

Q. Mr. Tourbikerider, "have you ever used performance enhancing drugs during your cycling career?"

A. "I have passed every drug test that I have taken."

Hmmm, sounds like a good denial. Does it meet the reticence rule? Nope, he never answered a simple yes or no question with a yes or no. I think most of us know how this one ended...

Q. Mr. Coach," "Are you sexually attracted to young boys?"

A. "Am I sexually attracted to young boys? Um, sexually attracted? I love young people, I love to be around young people, but I don't know if, no, I'm not sexually attracted to young boys."

Wow! If you can't figure this one out, we need a review! This answer violates every rule that we have discussed! I.E. Shortest answer is always the best answer, repeated the question, and did not follow the reticence rule. Looks like the answer of a child molester!

Q. Mr. Student, "We had a K-9 run on the lockers today. The K-9 alerted to the presence of gunpowder in your locker. Do you have any fireworks in your locker?"

A. "No"

Q. "Do you have a rifle in your locker?"

A. "No"

Q. "Do you have a pistol in your locker?"

A. "Not that I know of, there shouldn't be."

What's in the locker? That's right, the

answer that doesn't follow the reticence rule! Looks like someone has a pistol in their locker!

Q. "Honey, do you think I'm fat?"

A. "Baby, I love you just the way you are."

This is a no win situation, but it doesn't follow the reticence rule. Someone is fat and someone was deceptive in their answer!

Q. "Sir, did you have a sexual relationship with that intern?"

A. "I am not having a sexual

relationship with that intern."

Did he answer the question? No! The question was asking about the past, but his answer was in the present tense. Did he give us some great information? Yes!

Q. "Why did you murder your wife?"

A. "I had nothing to do with it."

Did the answer equal the question? Nope! An innocent person would have obviously stated, "I didn't murder my wife."

Q. "Mr. CEO, are you going to be laying any of us off?"

A. "We are looking at every possible way to streamline the company, so I wouldn't worry about that too much."

Did Mr. CEO answer this "yes" or "no" question with a "yes" or "no"? Sure didn't! Looks like there are some layoffs coming!

Q. "President, did you ask for the resignation of your Vice President?"

A. "I have received no resignation from the Vice President."

Did the President answer the question? Although his answer looks good, he did not answer the question that was asked. The President's answer in reference to this question leads one trained in lie detection to assume the Vice President is on the way out!

I'll stop with the examples, but I think you are getting it!

Please, if you get only one thing from this book, get the meaning of reticence! Once you understand, it will become so painfully easy to spot, you won't believe you didn't know this information earlier!

Knowing what reticence is, however, does not make you immune from doing your part. Your part is this: You MUST ask direct questions that illicit a yes or no response. I cannot stress this enough! No open ended questions!!! Remember, direct questions, direct questions, direct questions!!!!

Here is an example of asking an open-ended question and how it could possibly cause issues:

Question – "Hello Ms. Applicant, have you ever smoked marijuana or used cocaine?"

Answer - "When I was in college at a

party, someone was passing a joint around. Everybody was taking a puff, so I took one too. It was the only time in my life I tried the stuff and I didn't like it. I was young and just didn't use good judgment."

Well, what did you think of Ms. Applicant's response? She appears to be honest and open about her drug usage. She takes responsibility for her actions by telling us she used poor judgment. This type of lengthy answer can deceive an interviewer into thinking this person has completely answered the question.

The fact is, the person has neglected to answer the question in reference to cocaine use. Compound questions should be asked as two questions. First, ask, "Have you ever smoked marijuana?" Listen to the answer, and then ask follow up questions if necessary. Then ask the next question, "Have you ever used cocaine?" Listen to the answer.

How you ask questions is of enormous importance!

Along with the mistake of asking compound questions, here are some other mistakes I frequently observe:

Asking a question that answers itself. For example, "You don't know who did it, do you?" This is a terrible question! The answer is contained within the question. This type of question tells the subject that they do not know who did it. The only real question being asked is, "do you?" This form of question makes it very easy for the subject to answer with a "no." Since they have already been given the answer in the question, it is difficult to decide if they are lying or telling the truth. Your questions should always be straight forward, direct questions! Ask exactly what you want to know!

Another frequent (and costly) mistake I have observed often is to ask a question and then the interviewer will answer the question before the subject finishes their answer. The subject will begin to give an answer and then will hesitate. During this moment of silence, the interviewer will verbally finish the answer for him. All potential information is lost when the interviewer answers the questions for the subject. I have seen supposedly high-powered detectives in high profile cases make this mistake time and time again, totally destroying their chances of retrieving vital information from the subject being questioned. Don't make this mistake! Let them talk! The more they talk, the deeper they will dig their own hole!

When you are interviewing someone, think about how you are going to word your questions.

1. Do not ask compound questions! Compound questions make it easier for a person to avoid answering a question and harder for you to recognize that they did

not answer a question.

2. Your probing questions should be specific and to the point. When you ask questions that only allude to something, you give the person the opportunity to give you an honest answer without supplying the information you wanted.

3. If the subject gives a partial answer, show some patience. DO NOT finish the answer for them.

4. DO NOT give the subject the answer within the question.

Asking the proper questions is extremely important in determining if a person is telling the truth!

One other little technique that is extremely powerful: SILENCE. Silence is a great interviewing tactic. Some people feel they need to say something to break the silence.

It is your responsibility to ask direct questions!!!!

Remember: Direct Questions + Reticence = Successful Lie Detection!

Direct Questions + Reticence = Successful Lie Detection!

Direct Questions + Reticence = Successful Lie Detection!

Direct Questions + Reticence = Successful Lie Detection!

Direct Questions + Reticence = Successful Lie Detection!

CHAPTER 5

RED FLAG WORDS AND PHRASES

Now we will move to very important words and phrases that should always raise a "red flag" when speaking with, or interviewing an individual. These words and phrases should be stored in your memory. Before long, you will overhear a conversation or see a politician on television, and you will immediately pick up on deceptive words and phrases. It will scare you as to how deceitful, corrupt, and dishonest our leaders and others are, but at least you will not be caught unaware and "flat footed!"

Common Words or Phrases that you will frequently hear from a Deceptive Person:

I'm trying to tell the truth – What does the word "trying" mean? It means attempting, failing, not succeeding.

I'm telling you as much as possible – These words tell us that a person's honesty has limitations.

I Deny... – The word deny can mean to refuse to accept the truth.

I Intend – People have great intentions. Using the word does not mean the person will carry through.

All I know – When a person says "all I know," they are telling us they are limited in the knowledge about the situation.

All I Can Say – When a person says "all I can say," they are restricted by something other than their knowledge.

Confident – Just because someone is confident, that doesn't mean it will happen. An innocent person will say "I will."

NOTABLE WORDS:

BUT; YET; STILL; HOWEVER: Forget what is said before the word...the "real" statement follows!

ONLY: When emphasized, this is used as a denial or convincer.

SOMETIME: When is it?

ALWAYS/NEVER: Is this the real

world? Does something ALWAYS happen or NEVER happen? It's very rare.

EVERYBODY: Name one! Is EVERYBODY really doing _____?

OF COURSE: Answer? That's not an answer. Yes or no.

TRUST ME: Don't trust anybody!

GREAT LIES:

"Honestly"

"To be completely honest"

"Frankly"

"Truthfully"

"To tell the truth"

"Believe me"

"You're going to find this hard to believe"

"I wouldn't lie to you"

"Really"

"This really happened"

"I'm not kidding"

"I have to tell you"

"I wouldn't lie to you"

"I swear to God"

"I swear"

"To the best of my

recollection/knowledge"

"May God strike me dead"

"On my mother's grave"

"On my children's eyes"

"Noooooo, No, No, No, No" (multiple "No's" are always good!)

Another very important indicator that I always convey to my students is words that end in "LY." I cannot stress enough the importance of listening for words that end in LY. This is an indicator that I continually noticed the longer I studied and used lie detection at work.

After all of these years, this indicator is in my top 3 "go to" indicators for determining deception! Given time, you will hardly miss words ending in LY, and it will dawn on you, I'm becoming a human lie detector!

Bonus Information: "Three"- The Number 3

Three is a liar's number, no doubt about it! When deceptive people have to come up with a number, they will most often choose the number three. Why this is the case, no one can truly quantify, but I personally think it has something to do with the person's subconscious. Throwing out the number three keeps you from being "pinned down," and gives you an "out" or some "wiggle room" to help perpetuate the lie further, if needed, at a later date and time.

Additionally, in my experience, I have noticed that not only is three a liar's number, but also I have noticed that deceptive people usually use multiples of three as well. Don't ask me why, but I see it on a weekly basis! Keep your ears peeled for six, nine, 12, 15, etc. I'm telling you, it works!

CHAPTER 6

TOP TEN INDICATORS OF A LIAR

Proverbs 12:19

Truthful lips endure forever, but a lying tongue lasts only a moment...

#1. LIARS deviate from their normal behavior. A liar who speaks with pauses will suddenly become a rapid talker.

#2. LIARS are not proud about being deceitful and unconsciously lower their voice.

#3. LIARS repeat questions when asked (very good sign of deception) – buying time to think of an appropriate innocent response.

#4. LIARS deny specific aspects of a crime. A liar won't admit to stealing $1,000 if he or she stole $999.75.

#5. An innocent person's denial grows stronger over time and they get angry. LIARS don't get upset; they want to convince you that you are wrong about them.

#6. People often pause when LYING— giving them time to invent a story.

#7. LIARS are evasive. They will try to change the subject or gloss over a key point.

#8. A LIAR's verbal and non-verbal behavior are in conflict. They may say "No," but may be nodding "Yes."

#9. A lie is hard to remember. LIARS change their story over time.

#10. LIARS avoid eye contact. LIARS don't want to see the target of the lie.

CHAPTER 7
BODY LANGUAGE

As you have learned by now, I am not a huge fan of body language for detecting deception unless you have received formal training on the subject and have years of "real world" experience. I definitely feel that the "common man's" time would be much better spent in listening to words and statements in order to determine deception. However, this is not to say that body language does not have a definite place in the "common man's" arsenal of deception detection. There are some body language indicators that are simply too easy and effective to ignore. For this reason, I will add the most effective indicators, which, funny enough, are the easiest to detect! When you have some low-hanging fruit staring you right in the face, pick it!

With that being said, let's get started with body language!

Our fingers, hands, arms, legs, and their movements offer an interesting look into our true feelings. Most people aren't aware that their body speaks a language all its own and gives us, the lie detectors, clues to their deception. Try as they may to deceive us with their words, the truth can always be silently observed in the form of their body language. This is the very reason I added this chapter to the book. Body language is a great supplement to word and statement analysis and will make you a much more well-rounded lie detector.

A Liar's Eyes

Little or no eye contact is a classic sign of deception. A person who is lying to you will do almost anything to avoid making eye contact. Subconsciously they feel you will be able to see through them via their eyes. Feeling this subconscious guilt, the liar does not want to face you. Instead, they will glance down, or their eyes may dart from side to side. On the other hand, when we tell the truth or we're offended by a false accusation, we tend to give our full focus and have a fixed concentration on our accuser. We lock eyes with our accuser as if to say, "You're not getting away with this."

The Subconscious "Cover-Up"

If the hand goes straight to the face while a subject is responding to a direct question or when they are making a statement, this is often a sign of deception. The hand may cover their mouth while they are speaking, indicating that they really don't believe what they are saying to be true. The hand acts as a screen or filter to subconsciously attempt to hide their words.

Touching the nose is also considered a sign of deception, as well as scratching behind the ear or rubbing the eyes.

The Fake Smile

Deceptive expressions are often confined to the mouth area. A smile that's genuine lights up the whole face. When a smile is forced, the person's mouth is closed, tight, and there's no movement in the eyes or forehead. A smile that does not involve the whole face is a sign of deception.

While we're talking about fake smiles, be aware that the smile is the most common mask for emotion, because it best conceals the appearance in the lower face of anger, disgust, sadness, or fear. In other words, a person who doesn't want their true feelings to be revealed may "put on a happy face." Just a quick reminder—if the smile does not reflect the true emotion—happiness for example—it will not encompass the entire face.

The Posture of a Liar

When a person feels confident about a situation and conversation, they stand erect or sit up straight. This behavior also indicates how people feel about themselves in general. Those who are secure and confident stand tall, with shoulders back. Those who are insecure or unsure of themselves often stand hunched over, with their hands in their pockets.

Studies have shown that the best way to avoid being mugged is to walk briskly, with your head up and your arms moving. Such a style of moving conveys confidence. A conversation that produces feelings of confidence is normally a sign of truthfulness. A conversation that produces insecurity and weak body posture are normally signs of the subject being deceptive.

The Power of Touch

The person who is being deceitful will have little or no physical contact with the one they are talking to. This is an excellent and very reliable indicator of deception. While making a false statement or during a conversation containing one, the liar will rarely, if ever, touch the other person. Subconsciously, they are attempting to reduce the level of intimacy to help alleviate their guilt. Touch indicates psychological connection; it's used when we believe strongly in what we are saying.

Next time you watch a politician trying to garner votes with the public, watch as they touch people on the arm as they are shaking hands. They are subconsciously trying to convince the person that they are honest and have the courage of their convictions. Touch is also a subconscious way of imposing your dominance and intellect over another person. Hence, politicians are taught and love this technique.

As a side note, anytime I was in a volatile situation during a traffic stop or in any other less than ideal situation, I would speak to the person involved in a genuine, caring manner, and make sure to shake his or her hand and either hold his or her arm or pat him or her on the back. I know some in law enforcement would scoff at this gesture as lacking in officer safety, but it works great in diffusing the situation, and it kept me from receiving a single complaint despite thousands of contacts over the years.

Watch That Finger

Someone who is lying or hiding something will rarely, if ever, point a finger, either at others or straight up in the air. Finger pointing indicates conviction and authority, as well as the emphasis of a point. Someone who's not standing on solid ground probably won't be able to muster the audacity to finger point.

The Felony Yawn and Stretch

This is great indicator of deception and stress. I literally show this indicator to the classes I teach. I use copies of videos from traffic stops that have resulted in the seizure of various illegal items. The student can literally watch the subjects' reactions as I am searching their vehicle. Almost without fail, the subject will do the "felony yawn and stretch" at the moment I am finding the illegal items in question.

The same holds true in lying during an interview. When you get to a sensitive question and the subject displays the "felony yawn and stretch," you've got something!

Dry Mouth

I can't stress this one enough! There's not really much to say on this one. If you see the subject you are questioning licking their lips and asking for water, start taking notes! You're on to something!

Quick Reference Guide of Body Language

OPENNESS
1. Unbuttoned coat
2. Uncrossed Legs
3. Moving Closer
4. Uncrossed Arms

EVALUATION
1. Sitting on Edge of Chair
2. Body leaning forward
3. Hand on Cheek

4. Stroking Chin
5. Slow, careful cleaning of glasses

READINESS TO BUY
1. Sitting on Edge of Chair
2. Feet on tip toe
3. Standing, hands on hips
4. Rubbing palms together
5. Relaxed smile
6. Tugging at pants

DEFENSIVENESS
1. Arms crossed on chest
2. Fists clenched
3. Arms gripped
4. Leg over arm of chair
5. Sitting with chair reverted
6. Crossed legs
7. Face turned away

DOUBT
1. Pacing
2. Pinching bridge of nose
3. Lowered head

4. Hand over mouth
5. Rubbing eyes
6. Sideways glance
7. Rubbing nose

TENSION/DANGER
1. Short breaths
2. Tightly clenched hands
3. Wringing hands
4. Palm to back of neck
5. Clearing Throat
6. Fidgeting
7. Locking ankle
8. Removing hat
9. Grooming gestures
10. 100 yard stare

BOREDOM
1. Drumming on table
2. Head in hand
3. Drooping eyes
4. Doodling

CHAPTER 8

REVIEW

Everyone has the capability of determining if someone is being truthful or deceptive. In order to become proficient at discerning the truth, you MUST listen to what people are saying.

Did the Subject Answer the Question?

One of the first things we must notice is if the subject answered the question.

If you asked a "yes" or "no" question, did you get a "yes" or "no" answer?

People will usually give an answer

when asked a question. Look to see if they answered the specific question. If they didn't answer the question, there is something they are hiding. If you are the interviewer, ask the question again. Do not let the person get away without answering the question. Keep asking questions, and you will continue to obtain information from that person.

Look at the Language

Do not interpret what people are saying. People mean exactly what they are saying. Look at the specific words they are using. Ask yourself, "What is this person telling me?" If someone says, "I think I went to Jon's at 9:00," recognize that he did not tell you that he was at Jon's at 9:00. Also, look to see if people are specifically addressing the issue at hand or if they are talking about something else in an effort to lead you away from the truth.

There's a little riddle that can help keep your attention focused on what people are really saying and not interpret what they are saying.

Riddle: Three frogs are sitting on a log in the middle of a pond. One of the frogs says "Screw it, I'm tired of you guys," and decides to jump off the log. How many frogs are left on the log?

The answer is three. Just because the frog "decided" to jump off the log does not mean that he did. Hell, it doesn't even imply that he did, but I see people miss this answer all of the time. Make sure you are "in tune" with what people are really saying!

To drive home this "in tune" mindset,

I want to share a few statements that I have heard lately and show how we should "see through the noise" of someone's statement.

I read where the "leader" of an organization sent a message to all of the employees, lamenting problems within the organization and speaking about the peculiarities of fate. The leader spoke of a group that he was almost assigned to manage, but was instead assigned a different group to manage. Fast-forward a year and the group that he "almost" managed wound up being a disgrace and embarrassment of magnificent proportions. The leader spoke of fate, how he had tempted it, and told that the embarrassing group could have been his.

Let's think about this statement. Taken at face value, most people would probably just think, wow, he was lucky. The problem is, this statement tell us much more than meets the eye, very much more!

How many of you read this and thought, wow, not only is this guy not a leader, but he knows he's not! He is admitting that had he been the leader, the same result would have ensued. He doesn't have the mindset that if had he been the leader, none of this would have happened, because he would have provided the leadership and oversight that would have prevented this tragedy. Instead, he knew his leadership would have produced the same result. A true leader would have been thinking this entire statement would have never been made, as it would have been a non-issue!

Seeing "through the noise" and

listening to what people are "really" saying is such a powerful tool! This is the tool that enables you to rightly see the truth.

Another statement I read recently was somewhat similar. The "leader" of an organization was taking over for a leader that had recently left the organization. The leader sent a message to all of the employees saying that he had been hearing that the previous leader had failed to lead and that the organization was without a leader, similar to a large plane without a pilot. The leader then stated that he didn't necessarily agree with that assessment, but went on to advise that the organization now had a true leader that could make decisions.

Ask yourself, was all of that information needed? If he didn't "necessarily agree" with that information, why did he state it to everyone and then dismiss it? Was he taking a shot at the previous leader? Was he trying to put the previous leader down in order to bolster his leadership? The fact is, it shows immaturity and a lack of self-esteem. We are all aware that when people put others down in order to make themselves look better, they usually have low self-worth and self-esteem. Much can be seen in this statement if you will listen to what people are "truly" saying. I feel sorry for this organization!

The last example that I have recently observed was from a preacher on television. As I was flipping through the channels, I noticed one of the "send me money" preachers, and I just had to watch for a few minutes. The preacher was really trying to make a point and kept telling his audience, "listen, listen, this is a true story, listen."

Now what in the world does it tell us when a preacher is telling us to listen because this is a true story! What kind of stories does he usually tell? Why preface your story with "this one is true?" This statement has so many issues with it, I would be leery to believe anything this guy ever said or preached!

Are you getting it? See "through the noise" and hear what people are "truly" saying.

Look for Words and Phrases that Indicate Deception

Remember that people will try to convince you of their truthfulness by using certain phrases as an added emphasis. Always remember phrases such as "I swear to God," "To tell the truth," "To be completely honest," and "I wouldn't lie to you."

Also, keep your ears peeled for those words that end in LY!

Keep your ears peeled for the number three (3) and any multiples of the number three (3).

Always pay attention to the words "really" and "trying." I can't tell you how many times I have heard these words when talking to, or interviewing, a liar! Think for a minute about the word "trying." Trying means attempting, failing, and not succeeding.

Keep focused on the words BUT, YET, STILL and HOWEVER—forget what is said before the word; the "real" statement follows!

Look for Unnecessary Words and Stuttering

"I, I, I, um, I um." We can also find unnecessary words in the form of stuttering. Stuttering when answering a sensitive question is a sign of deception.

What Hasn't the Subject Told You?

Think about it. People will leave out certain information from their story. Usually, they leave this information out because the information incriminates them or they are trying to lead you in another direction. Listen, but do not interpret. People's words will betray them!

Did the Subject Answer the Question with a Question?

This indicates that the person in thinking about their answer. They have information to tell, but are uncertain how much they should tell you. Therefore, they may repeat the question in order to buy themselves some additional time to think of a good answer. If you fail to ask the question again, they will get away with not answering the question. Even if they eventually answer the question, you know they are withholding some information that you want to obtain.

Watch how you Phrase the Questions

DO NOT ask compound questions! Compound questions make it easy for the person to withhold information. They may not answer one of the questions, and you could possibly miss it. Ask your questions one at a time. Also, do not give them the answer within the question. "You didn't do it, did you?" is a terrible question. NEVER answer the question for them and do not anticipate what their answer will be. Allow them to state whatever they want to say.

How would You answer the Question?

Finally, this is common sense! Ask yourself how you would answer a certain question, or how you would respond to a certain allegation. By comparing your answer with their answer, you can sometimes gain insight into what people are telling you and what they are not telling you. Getting to the truth is not that hard if you will just listen to what people are saying!

Last, but Not Least—RETICENCE!

Reticence: Does Their Answer Equal the Question You Asked???

Always Remember:

Direct Questions + Reticence = Successful Lie Detection!

CLOSING

As I hope you can see, detecting a liar can be MADE EASY.

I hope you have enjoyed the book and learned a thing or two about detecting lies and deception.

Whether it's business, work, or personal matters—from casual conversations to full blown interrogations—the techniques that you have learned in this book will make you a better interpreter of deception. Having these skills will give you more confidence, relevance, and will allow you to make better and more informed decisions. Having the edge in your decision-making can have positive, far-reaching implications for you and your family in future years.

Now that you've gained this extra edge, you'll enjoy the freedom of advancing your business and personal relationships, without the fear of feeling paranoid, fooled, or embarrassed.

There will most likely never be a way to stop people from lying to you. In fact, I would go so far as to say that being lied to will increase in the years to come. However, you will now be equipped to deal with people that will inevitably try to deceive you. With each new encounter, YOU will have the edge!

At the end of the day, this isn't rocket science. KEEP IT SIMPLE!

DIRECT QUESTIONS + RETICENCE = LIE DETECTION!!!!

Good Luck and Stay Safe!

ABOUT THE AUTHOR

The author is currently employed as a State Trooper with a state in the Mid-South, holding the earned rank of Captain/Troop Commander.

He holds degrees in both Criminal Justice and Business, as well as a Master's Degree in Business Management. He is also an expert in Body Language and Statement Analysis.

Some of his notable achievements are as follows:

"Top Gun" Award winner and voted class representative of Police Academy.

Certified K-9 Handler

DEA/DIAP Federal Criminal Interdiction Instructor

DEA Distinguished Achievement Award

DIAP Distinguished Instructor Award

Expert Witness for state in reference to Criminal Interdiction, Body Language, and Statement Analysis

Has seized in excess of $25,000,000.00 in cash and drugs

4X Criminal Interdictor of the Year Award Winner

2X Criminal Interdiction Team of the Year Award Winner

Delta Mu Delta member

Leadership Academy Instructor

Designated as State Strategic National Stockpile Commander

University Adjunct Instructor – Instructs courses in Organizational Behavior, Organizational Leadership, Criminal Justice and Ethics

In his free time, he enjoys spending time with his family, traveling, enjoying his kids' sports, and the outdoors, especially Colorado. He also enjoys hunting, fishing, Baylor baseball, and Slipknot!

Made in the USA
San Bernardino, CA
27 January 2013